LET'S GET OUTDOORS!
Kayaking
by Lisa Owings
BLASTOFF! 2 READERS
BELLWETHER MEDIA • MINNEAPOLIS, MN

Blastoff! Readers are carefully developed by literacy experts to build reading stamina and move students toward fluency by combining standards-based content with developmentally appropriate text.

Level 1 provides the most support through repetition of high-frequency words, light text, predictable sentence patterns, and strong visual support.

Level 2 offers early readers a bit more challenge through varied sentences, increased text load, and text-supportive special features.

Level 3 advances early-fluent readers toward fluency through increased text load, less reliance on photos, advancing concepts, longer sentences, and more complex special features.

★ Blastoff! Universe

Reading Level

Grade K

Grades 1–3

Grade 4

This edition first published in 2023 by Bellwether Media, Inc.

Library of Congress Cataloging-in-Publication Data

LC record for Kayaking available at: https://lccn.loc.gov/2022038737

Editor: Rebecca Sabelko Series Design: Andrea Schneider Book Designer: Laura Sowers

Printed in the United States of America, North Mankato, MN.

Table of Contents

What Is Kayaking?

Kayaking is traveling in a kayak. Kayaks are small boats often with covered tops.

Kayakers sit low in **cockpits**. They use **paddles** with two **blades** to move and **steer**.

Some people race in kayaks.
Others fish or hunt.
Many people just like to paddle.

Favorite Kayaking Spot

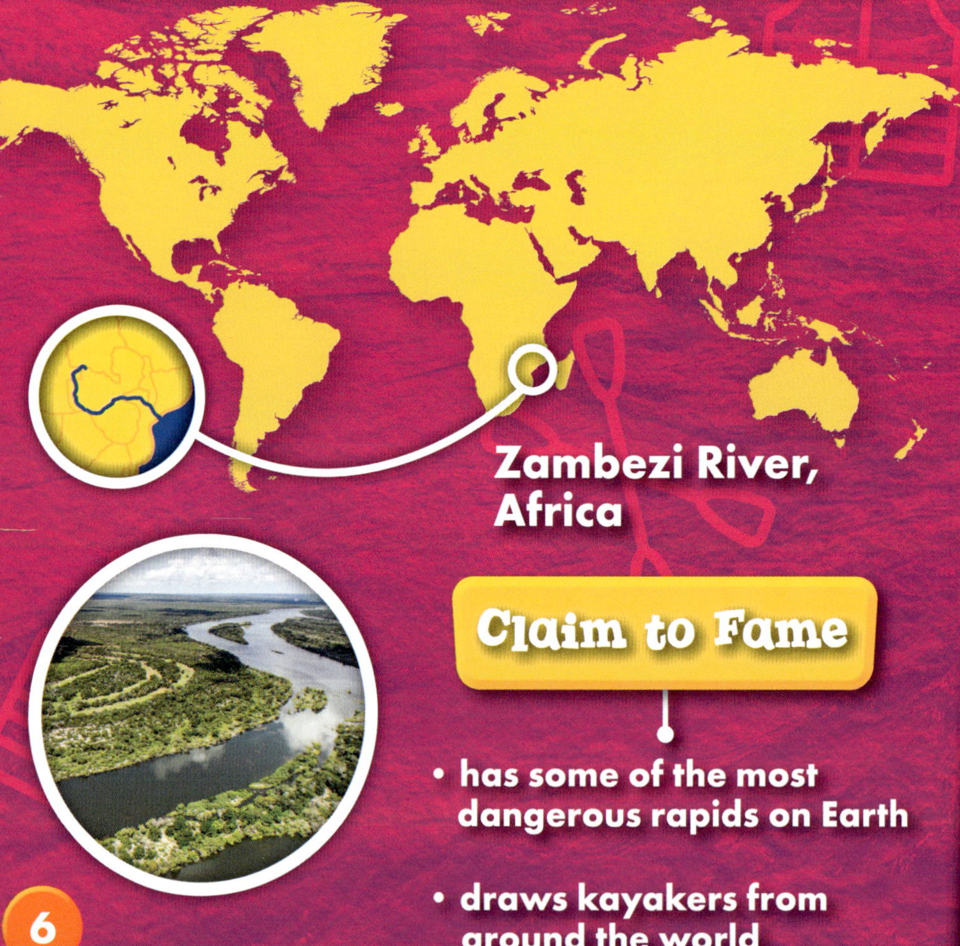

Claim to Fame

- has some of the most dangerous rapids on Earth
- draws kayakers from around the world

river rapids

Kayakers can explore calm lakes, wild river **rapids**, or open oceans.

Getting Started Kayaking

Kayakers find a calm beach to **launch** from. They set up their seats and **foot pegs**.

Friends can help kayakers climb in and push off.

Kayakers make forward **strokes** to go straight. They move each blade from front to back.

Sweep strokes turn kayaks.

Paddle Strokes

forward stroke

sweep stroke

reverse stroke

draw stroke

New kayakers can explore lakes and calm rivers.

Guided **tours** are safe ways to try rapids or ocean waters.

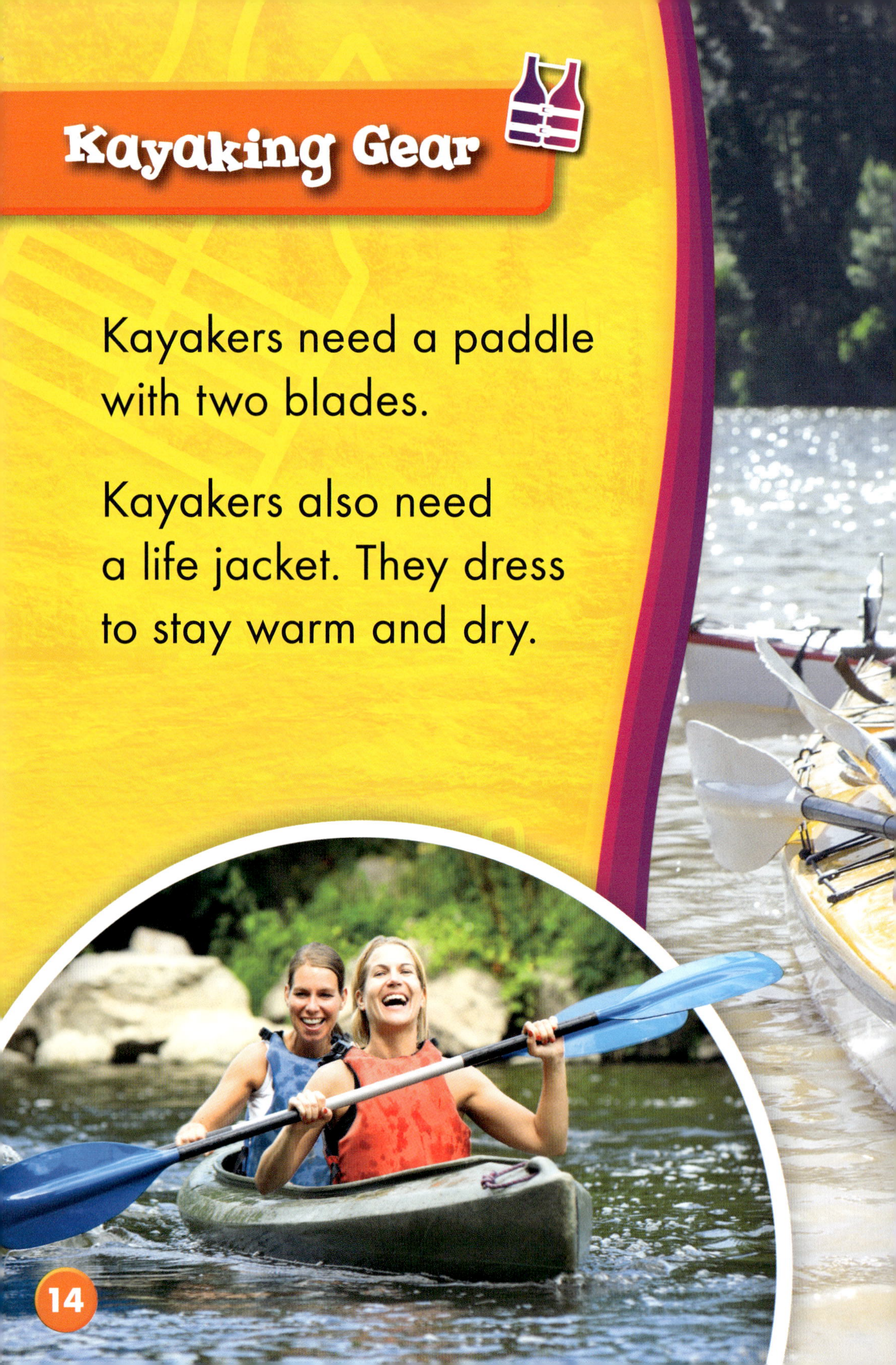

Kayaking Gear

Kayakers need a paddle with two blades.

Kayakers also need a life jacket. They dress to stay warm and dry.

life jackets

Spray skirts keep water out of kayaks. Kayakers can remove water with a **bilge pump**.

Kayaking Gear

Waterproof bags keep supplies dry.

Kayaking Safety

Kayakers should always explore with others. They must keep their life jackets on.

Rough water can be dangerous. Helmets protect heads.

Beginning kayakers should stay near shore. They can swim their boat in if it tips. Skilled kayakers can **roll** a tipped kayak.

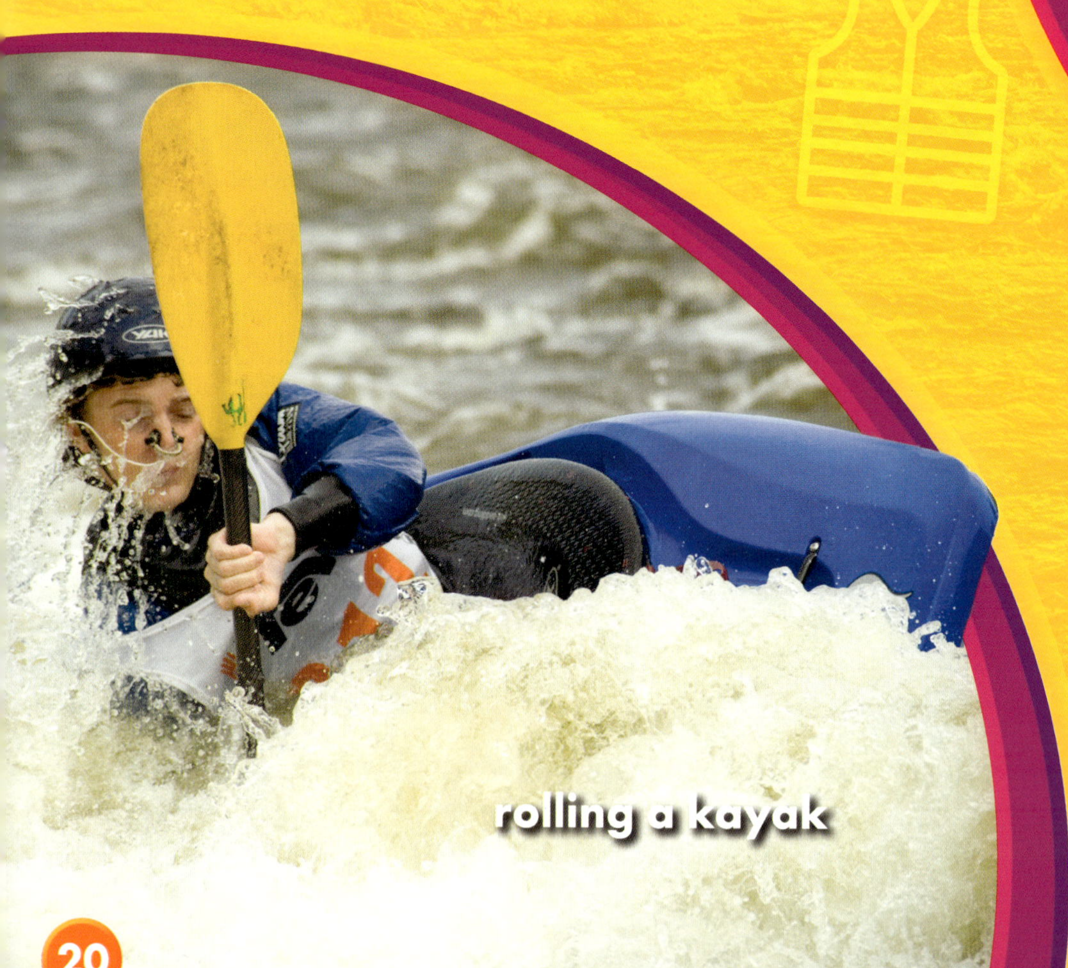

rolling a kayak

Getting wet and cold means it is time to paddle in!

Glossary

bilge pump—a tool that removes water that collects in the bottom of a kayak

blades—wide, flat surfaces on paddles

cockpits—areas in kayaks where kayakers sit

foot pegs—flat objects to place feet against while paddling

launch—to move a boat into water

paddles—tools with long handles and flat blades that are used to move boats

rapids—rough, fast-moving parts of a river

roll—to right an upside-down kayak without getting out

spray skirts—waterproof covers that fit around kayakers and the openings of kayaks to keep water out

steer—to guide the movement of something

strokes—paddle movements that move a boat

sweep—related to wide, C-shaped paddle strokes that turn boats

tours—group trips to learn about new places

waterproof—made of material that keeps water out

To Learn More

AT THE LIBRARY

Green, Sara. *Rivers*. Minneapolis, Minn.: Bellwether Media, 2022.

Laden, Nina. *Yellow Kayak*. New York, N.Y.: Simon & Schuster Books for Young Readers, 2018.

Owings, Lisa. *Canoeing*. Minneapolis, Minn.: Bellwether Media, 2023.

ON THE WEB

FACTSURFER

Factsurfer.com gives you a safe, fun way to find more information.

1. Go to www.factsurfer.com.
2. Enter "kayaking" into the search box and click 🔍.
3. Select your book cover to see a list of related content.

Index

The images in this book are reproduced through the courtesy of: Windzepher, front cover; marekuliasz, p. 3; Max Topchii, pp. 4-5; kali9, p. 5; Anton_Ivanov, p. 6; Getmilitaryphotos, pp. 6-7; Razvan Dima, p. 8; Pat Shearman/ Alamy, pp. 8-9; maki_shmaki, pp. 10-11; JaySi, p. 11 (forward stroke); Virrage Images, p. 11 (sweep stroke); MemoriesStocker, p. 11 (reverse stroke); WoodysPhotos, p. 11 (draw stroke); All Canada Photos/ Alamy, pp. 12-13; Corepics VOF, p. 14; Juice Flair, pp. 14-15; Andrew McCandlish/ Alamy, p. 16; Vitaliy Kyrychuk, pp. 16-17; Monkey Business Images, pp. 18-19; Helioscribe, p. 19; Bailey-Cooper Photography/ Alamy, p. 20; anek.soowannaphoom, pp. 20-21; New Africa, p. 23.